A Note to Parents

DK READERS is a compelling new program for beginning readers, designed in conjunction with leading literacy experts, including Dr. Linda Gambrell, Director of the School of Education at Clemson University. Dr. Gambrell has served on the Board of Directors of the International Reading Association and as President of the National Reading Conference.

Beautiful illustrations and superb full-color photographs combine with engaging, easy-to-read stories to offer a fresh approach to each subject in the series. Each DK READER is guaranteed to capture a child's interest while developing his or her reading skills, general knowledge, and love of reading.

The five levels of DK READERS are aimed at different reading abilities, enabling you to choose the books that are exactly right for your child:

Pre-level 1: Learning to read
Level 1: Beginning to read
Level 2: Beginning to read alone
Level 3: Reading alone
Level 4: Proficient readers

W9-BDM-811

The "normal" age at which a child begins to read can be anywhere from three to eight years old, so these levels are intended only as a general guideline.

No matter which level you select, you can be sure that you are helping your child learn to read, then read to learn!

LONDON, NEW YORK, MUNICH,
MELBOURNE, AND DELHI

Editor Dawn Sirett
Art Editor Jane Horne
Senior Editor Linda Esposito
Senior Art Editor
Diane Thistlethwaite
US Editor Regina Kahney
Production Melanie Dowland
Picture Researcher Andrea Sadler
Natural History Consultant
Theresa Greenaway
Reading Consultant
Linda B. Gambrell, Ph.D.

First American Edition, 1999
07 08 09 10 9 8 7 6 5 4
Published in the United States by DK Publishing, Inc.
375 Hudson Street, New York, New York 10014

Published in Great Britain by Dorling Kindersley Limited.

Library of Congress Cataloging-in-Publication Data
Moses, Brian, 1950-
    Munching, crunching, sniffing & snooping / by Brian Moses. -- 1st
American ed.
        p.   cm. -- (Dorling Kindersley readers. Level 2)
    Summary: Describes the various ways different animals use their
mouths and noses.
    ISBN-13: 978-0-7894-4753-1 (hb)
    ISBN-13: 978-0-7894-4752-4 (pb)
    1. Mouth Juvenile literature. 2. Nose Juvenile literature.
[1. Mouth. 2. Nose. 3. Animals.] I. Title. II. Title: Munching,
crunching, sniffing, and snooping. III. Series.
QL857.M359 1999
591.4--dc21   99-20404
                                       CIP
                                        AC

Color reproduction by Colourscan, Singapore
Printed and bound in China by L Rex Printing Co., Ltd.
The publisher would like to thank the following for
their kind permission to reproduce their photographs:
Key: t=top, b=bottom, l=left, r=right, c=center
Colorific: 24 c; **Innerspace Visions**: Marty Snyderman 14 tl; **Frank
Lane Picture Agency**: S. Jonasson 26 br; **London Zoo**: 29 c; **Oxford Scientific
Films**: 26 tr, Alan Root 17 tr; **Planet Earth Pictures**: 5 br, 16 tl; Brian Kenney
28 bc; **Frank Spooner Pictures**: 24 br; **Tony Stone Images**: Charley A.
Mauzy, Colin Prior front cover background; ©**Barrie Watts**: 5 t; ©**Jerry
Young**: 3 c, 7 bl, 9 cr, 10 tl, 10 br, 13 tr, 15 br, 21 br, 23 c, 25 tl, 25 cr, 32 tl.
Additional credits:
Kenneth Lilly (illustrator); Margherita Gianni (jacket designer);
Gary Staab (model maker); Peter Anderson, Paul Bricknell, Geoff
Brightling, Jane Burton, Gordon Clayton, Geoff Dann, Neil Fletcher,
Steve Gorton, Frank Greenaway, Dave King, Bill Ling, Karl Shone, Steve
Shott, Kim Taylor, David Ward, Jerry Young (photography for DK).
All other images © Dorling Kindersley Limited
For further information see: www.dkimages.com

Discover more at
www.dk.com

DK READERS

BEGINNING TO READ ALONE
2

Munching, Crunching, Sniffing, and Snooping

Written by Brian Moses

DK
DK Publishing, Inc.

Mouths are for eating,
drinking, and speaking.

Mouths are for
tasting, biting,
and licking.

Mouths are for
sipping, chewing,
and smiling.

Mouths are for singing,
blowing, and kissing.

Mouths are for
SHOUTING,

whispering,

and *YAWNING.*

Whose mouths are these?

The king of beasts roams the plain.
He has big, sharp teeth
and a long, shaggy mane.

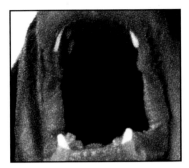

Tell her to sit.
Tell her to lie.
She wags her tail
and jumps up high!

He likes to leap.
He likes to hop.
He dives into ponds.
Splash! Plop! Plop!

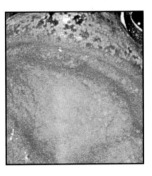

Long and low
with scaly skin,
he lies in water
up to his chin!

Were you right? Turn the page …

We open our mouths to talk …

but a lion
roars …

RRRRR!
RRRRR!

a dog barks …

WOOF

WOOF

CROAK

a frog croaks ...

and an alligator smiles.
But he's not really smiling.
He's ready to
snap up animals
that come to the river
for a drink.

Body talk
As well as making noises
with their mouths,
many animals "talk"
with their bodies and tails.
This dog wants to play.

Mom says, "Don't stick your tongue out."

But a chameleon (kuh-MEEL-yun) flicks out a long tongue that sticks to an insect like flypaper.

Sharp shooter
A chameleon's tongue shoots out like a spring. Catching insects is tricky. Baby chameleons often miss.

A cat uses her
rough tongue
like a comb
to lick and clean
her fur.

A gecko can clean
his own eyes with
his long tongue.

Dad says, "Don't stand there with your mouth wide open."

Try telling that to a snake who is trying to swallow an egg ...

or a howler monkey who's warning others not to come too close ...

or a hyena
who won't
stop laughing.

The hyena's laugh
is no joking matter.
Hyenas make
this sound
when they hunt
and kill their prey.

Mighty biters
Spotted hyenas
have very strong jaws
that can crush and chew
large bones and horns.
Even lions can't do this.

Mom says, "Brush your teeth."

But some sharks
don't need toothbrushes.
Small fish clean their teeth for them.

A hamster's strong teeth
never stop growing.
So he doesn't care
about tooth decay.

A turtle never has to worry
about losing her teeth
because she hasn't got any!
Instead, the edges of her jaws
are hard and bony.

Underwater fishing

An alligator snapping turtle's
tongue looks like a worm.
When she opens her mouth,
fish think they see dinner.
They swim in and get snapped up!

A bird's mouth
is called a beak.
Birds use their beaks
to collect food
and then eat it.

A heron
has a long,
pointed beak
for catching fish.

A parrot's beak
is so strong
that she can
crack open nuts.

A woodpecker can dig for insects in tree trunks with his sharp beak.

Noses are for smelling,
sniffing, and snooping.

Noses are for breathing,
sneezing, and snorting.

Noses are for nuzzling up to Mom, for finding food, and for staying out of danger.

Noses are for poking ...

but not for picking! Ugh!

Whose noses are these?

In Chinese forests she's top bear.
She's black and white
and very rare.

This animal swings
from tree to tree.
He has fingers and toes
like you and me.

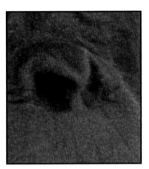

She digs out tunnels
under the ground
and pushes the earth
into a mound.

He's big and white.
He lives in the snow.
He's covered in fur
from head to toe.

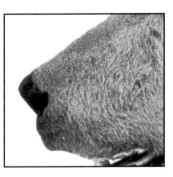

Were you right? Turn the page …

Animals have a stronger
sense of smell than we do.
It helps them to find food.

A panda
sniffs out bamboo,
which is her
favorite food.

An orangutan
uses his nose
to find the
ripest fruit.

A mole sniffs out
earthworms in the dark ...

and polar bears sniff out seals
that are hiding in the snow.

Sniffing for our supper
People use pigs to sniff out
truffles under the ground.
Truffles are like mushrooms,
but they cost a lot more because
they are very hard to find.

Mom says, "Don't be nosy."

But police officers never tell
their dogs to stop nosing around.

Smelly clues

Police dogs can
track down criminals
by sniffing small traces
of human sweat.

An echidna pokes
his long nose
between rocks,
looking for ants.

Bears stick their noses into beehives
in search of honey.
Their fur protects them
from most bee stings,
but sometimes
they get stung
on the nose!

Dad says, "Use a hanky to wipe your nose."

You wouldn't say this to sea birds because they don't carry handkerchiefs … but they do have runny noses.

Sea birds take in a lot of salt as they feed. Later it comes out through their noses as very salty water.

A camel never has a runny nose.
She can close her nostrils
to keep liquid in and sand out.
This helps her to live
in the hot, dry desert.

Mom says, "If you don't bathe, you'll stink."

But some animals stink on purpose.

Skunks can spray a smelly liquid at their enemies. The liquid comes from stink glands under their bushy tails.

Aim and fire!
A spotted skunk squirts
his evil-smelling spray
by lifting up his tail
and doing a handstand.

Jaguars eat a lot of turtles.
These small animals
are usually easy
to catch.

But this tiny turtle can give off
such an awful smell
that jaguars leave her alone.
No wonder she is called
a stinkpot turtle!

Dad says,
"Don't turn your nose up
at your vegetables."

But you wouldn't
say this to
an elephant.

An elephant's long nose
is called a trunk.
She turns it up to collect leaves to eat.

She can use it
to lift a log,
suck up water
for a shower,
hold on to another elephant's tail ...
or make a loud noise called trumpeting.

More Fascinating Facts

Female alligators can help their eggs hatch by gently rolling the eggs in their mouths.

When a hippo yawns, he is really warning off other hippos by showing them his huge teeth.

Dogs and cats can carry their young in their mouths without hurting them. They pick up each baby by the scruff of its neck.

A hamster can fill his mouth with lots of food. He stuffs the food in his cheeks, then carries it to his nest, where he stores it for later.

An elephant's trunk can lift a big log, but it can also pick up tiny things, such as a single leaf.

A male emperor moth can smell a female several miles away.

Salmon are able to smell their way back to the stream where they were hatched.

A snake smells and tastes the air with her tongue. She flicks it in and out to tell whether food, a mate, or an enemy is near.